Contents

Resource Pages:

Activity Pages:

Insert:

16 full color picture cards
12 full color pattern cards
(Teacher will need to cut these cards apart.)

D1606827

Describe It!

You can train children to be more observant by doing activities in which children must look carefully and then describe what they see. Discuss the various ways objects can be described (color, size, shape, use, material it is made of, taste, location).

A. Brown Bag Riddles:

Give each child a brown lunch bag containing an object. Keep the items simple for younger students. The child looks in the bag and describes what he/she sees. The other children try to guess what is in the bag.

Example: I see something round. It is blue and white. It is made of rubber. It can bounce. What is it? (ball)

B. Alike and Different:

Show children two objects that are similar in two or more ways. They are to describe how the objects are alike. They then describe how the objects are different.

Example: a slice of brown bread and a graham cracker
a round cookie and a rice cracker
a quarter and a dime
a flag and a handkerchief
a clock and a wristwatch

C. Use Picture Cards:

Remove the picture cards from the center of the book. Cut the cards apart to use with the following activities.

1. Give a child a card to describe. Display that card and two or three others. The children must try to select the card that was described.

2. Show several of the picture cards. Discuss the order with your students. Mix the cards up and select a child to put them in the same order.

Who Do I See?

A. Have three children come to the front of the classroom. The rest of the children in class close their eyes. The teacher describes one of the three children standing in front of the room. The other children open their eyes and try to decide which child was described.

Variations:

The teacher or a student describes someone in the classroom. The other students try to decide who it is.

Describe someone in the school who is not present in the room.

Describe someone from T.V. or from a story.

B. Find a picture in a magazine that contains three or more people. Select someone to describe one person in the picture. The other players try to guess who has been described.

Variation:

Have children draw pictures of someone (real or fiction) to use in playing the game. Put the pictures on a bulletin board for everyone to see. Select a child to describe his/her picture. The other players try to find the picture described.

Changes

A. What Is Missing?

Place several objects on a table. (As you increase the number of objects, the task becomes more difficult.) Name all the items for your students. They close their eyes while you remove one or more items. The players then open their eyes and try to decide which item was removed.

You can also play the game using the picture cards provided with this book. Younger children will find this more difficult than using real objects.

B. The Order Of Things

Place several objects in a row. (Remember, the more objects you use, the harder the task.) Name the items in order several times. Children close their eyes while you make one or more changes in the order of the objects. The players open their eyes and try to put the items back in the correct order.

You can play the game using the picture cards provided in this book.

C. Build A Pattern:

Give children paper circles, squares, and triangles. Show one of the pattern cards provided in this book. The children are to copy the pattern on their desk tops.

You can make the task more difficult by asking children to show what would come next in the pattern or to do the pattern in reverse.

Use the shape pattern cards with the worksheet on page 23. Use the animal pattern cards with the worksheet on page 24. Each of the pages can be used more than once by selecting different pattern cards each time.

A good source of material to practice visual skills is *Shape and Color Activity Cards* by EVAN-MOOR.

Let's Play A Game

A. Do As I Do:

The teacher or a student is the leader. Everyone else copies the motions demonstrated. Start with one or two easy movements. Gradually add a greater number and/or more difficult motions as students become better able to follow.

Examples:

- Touch different parts of your body.

- Put your hands over your head, behind your back, in front of your body, etc.

- Swing your arms in opposition.

- Act out an activity such as washing a window, eating a banana, or making a sandwich.

- Hop around in a small circle on one foot.

B. I Spy:

This game can be played in the classroom or sitting outside on the lawn. Remind children of all the different ways they can describe an object (size, color, shape, etc.) before beginning the game.

Example:

- I spy something that is made of cloth. It has four sides. It has stars and stripes. (flag)

- I spy something coming down the street. It is big and shiny. It has hoses and ladders. It makes a loud noise as it races down the street. (fire truck)

C. Charades:

Select someone to demonstrate a motion. The other players must guess what the motion represents. Be sure that all the players understand that they are to act out something the class can recognize.

Example:
- sweep the floor
- do a dance
- paint a wall
- pour a drink
- take a bath

 Visual Perception Skills

Let's Take A "Looking" Walk

Take advantage of good weather to take a "looking" walk to practice visual perception skills.

Choose a location:

1. the school yard
2. the neighborhood
3. a local park
4. a business area
5. a zoo or animal shelter
6. a beach, pond, lake, or river area
7. a museum or aquarium

Set a "looking" task:

1. look for people (working, playing)
2. look for animals
3. look for types of buildings
4. look for signs
5. look for types of vehicles
6. look for objects of a certain color or shape
7. look for plants

When you return to school, discuss what has been seen. You may also have children illustrate what they have seen.

On rainy or snowy days you can line up by the windows and look for specific items instead of going outside for a walk.

Visual Perception Skills

Draw What I Draw

Guided drawing is an enjoyable and successful way to help children practice visual perception skills. They must watch carefully to see what details to include in their pictures. Drawing also helps children develop greater small muscle control and improve their ability to follow auditory and visual directions.

Teacher may draw on the chalkboard or use an overhead projector. Provide children with large sheets of paper and either pencils or crayons and you are ready to begin.

Select simple forms to draw in the beginning.

Draw each picture one step at a time. Allow adequate time for children to copy each step.

When the basic picture has been completed, allow time for students to add something of their own to the drawing.

Another source of drawing lessons is *Art Moves the Basics Along Animal Units* by EVAN-MOOR.

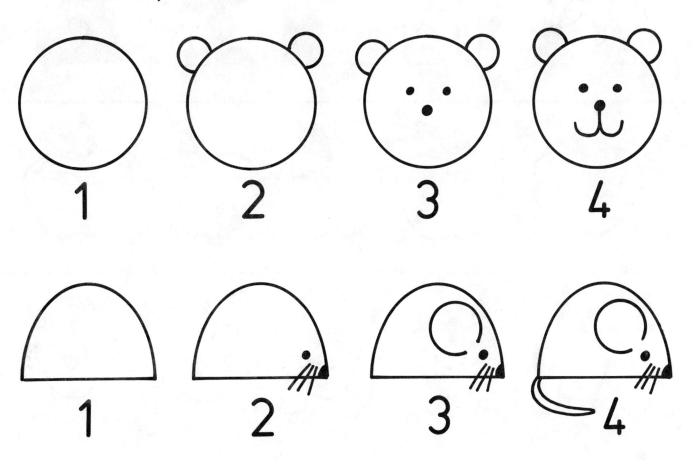

Visual Perception Skills

Teacher: Children are to circle the two pictures that are the same in each row.

Which Are The Same?

8

Visual Perception Skills

Which One Is Different?

9 Visual Perception Skills

Match

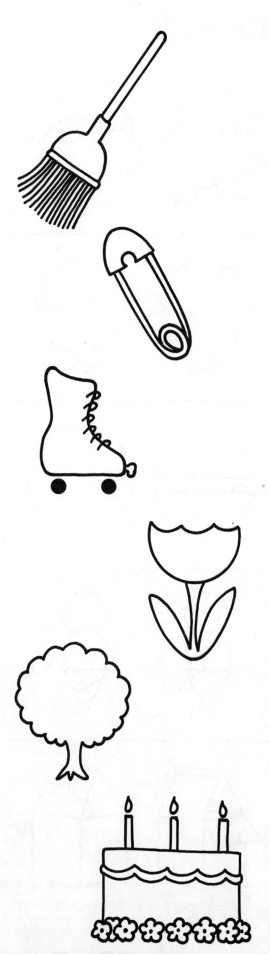

10 Visual Perception Skills

Match

11   Visual Perception Skills

Find the Animals

12

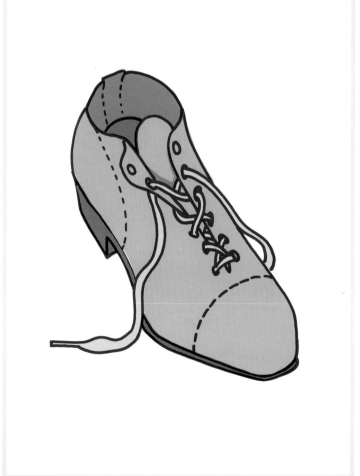

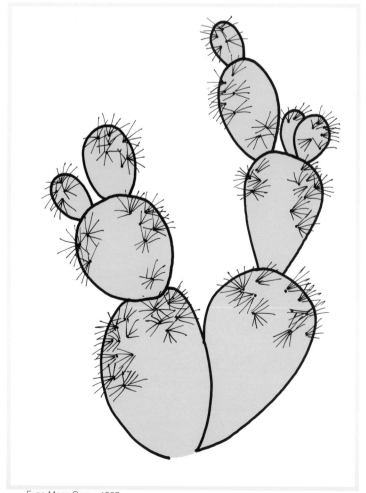

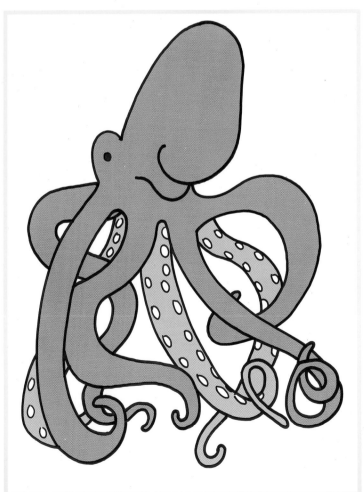

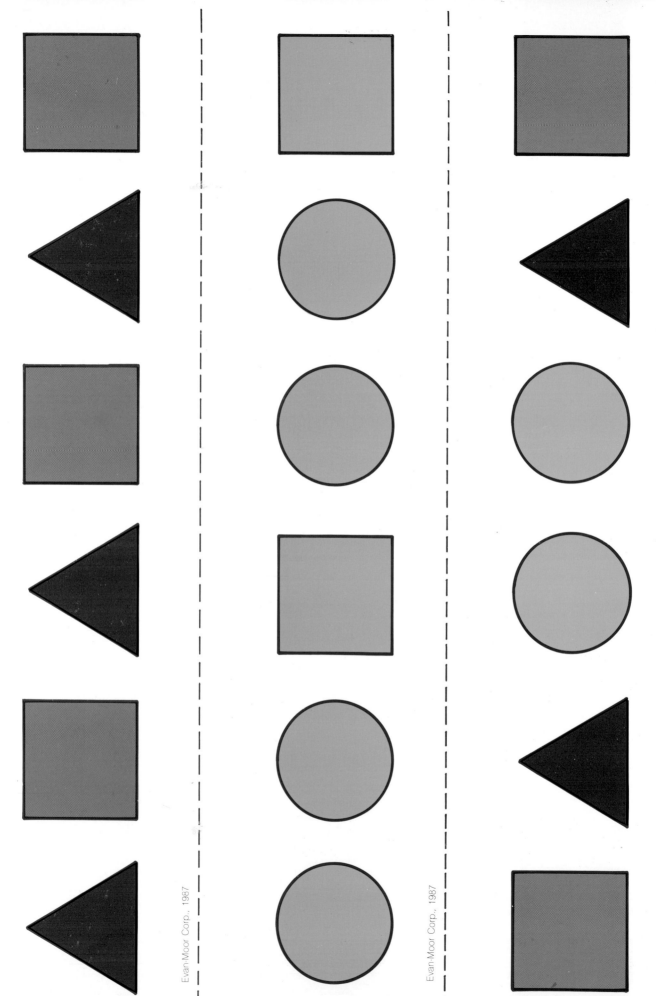

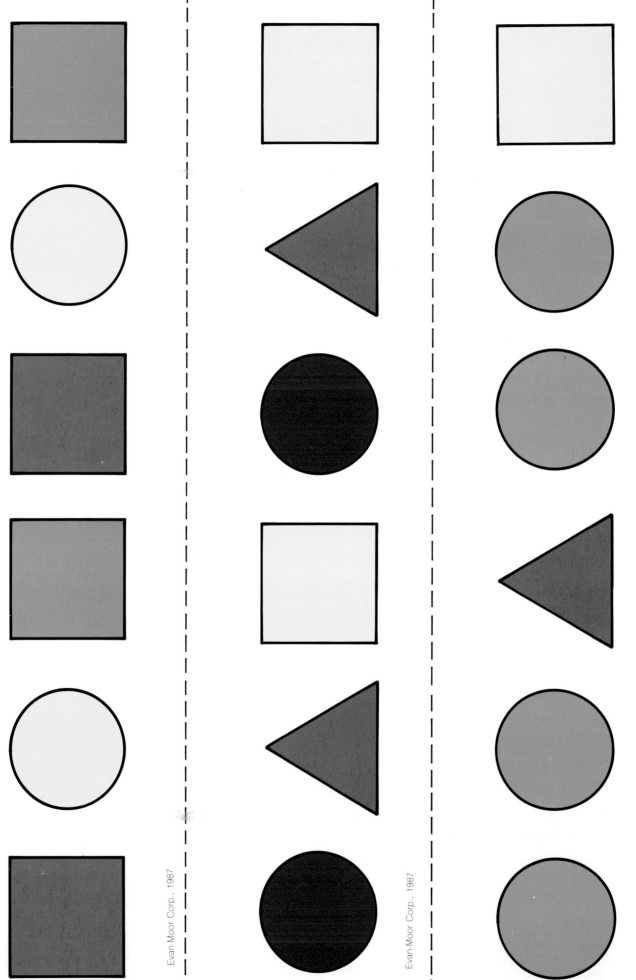

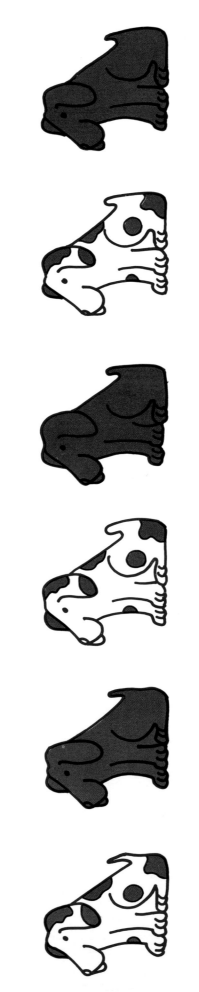

Evan-Moor Corp., 1987

Evan-Moor Corp., 1987

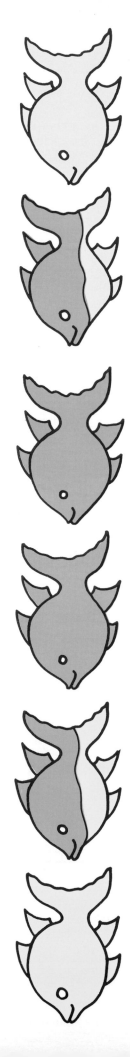

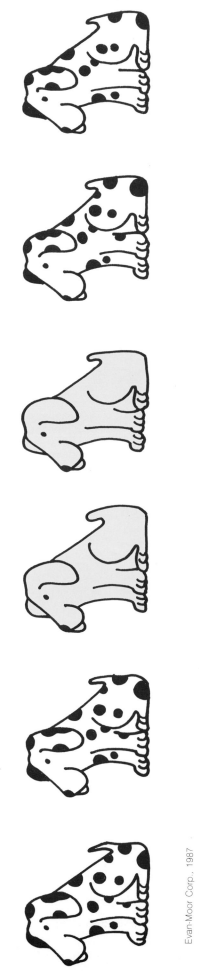

Find the Toys

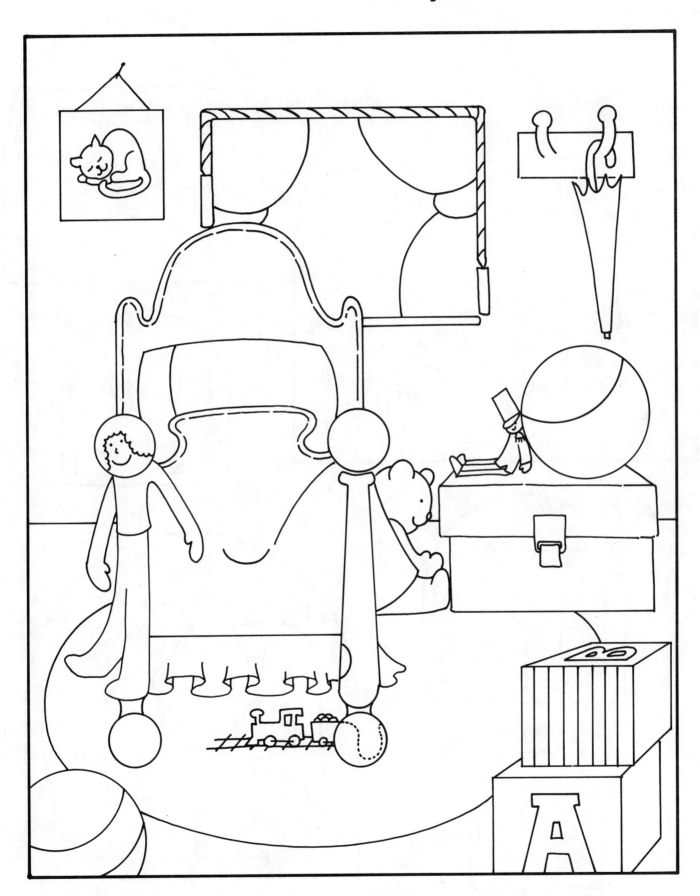

Visual Perception Skills

The Elephant Parade

14

Visual Perception Skills

School Bus

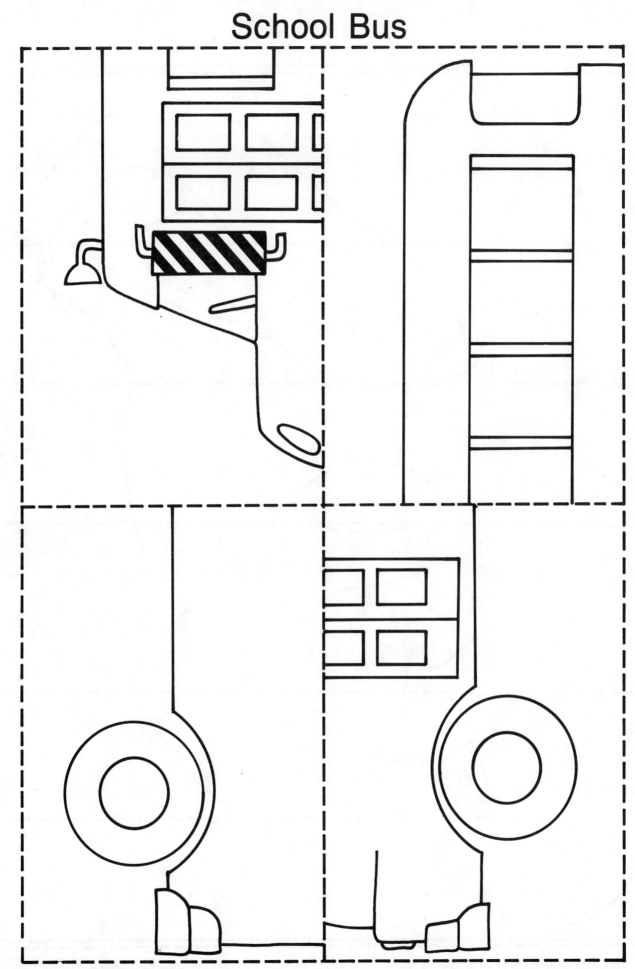

Dinosaur

16 Visual Perception Skills

Complete the Picture

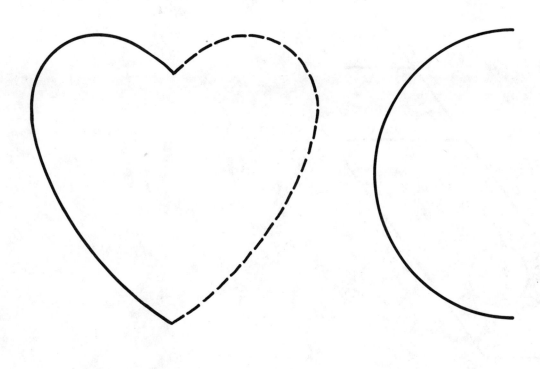

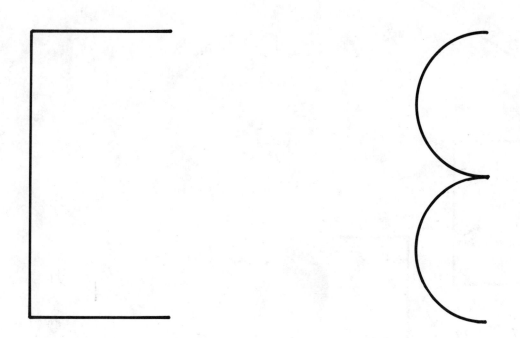

Complete the Picture

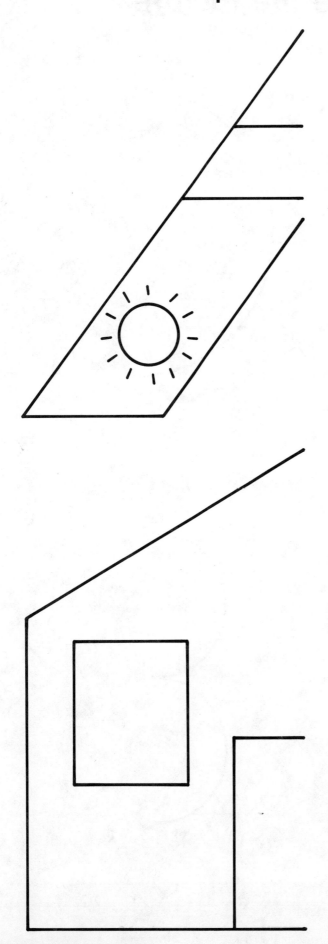

18

Visual Perception Skills

Lines...Dots...Circles

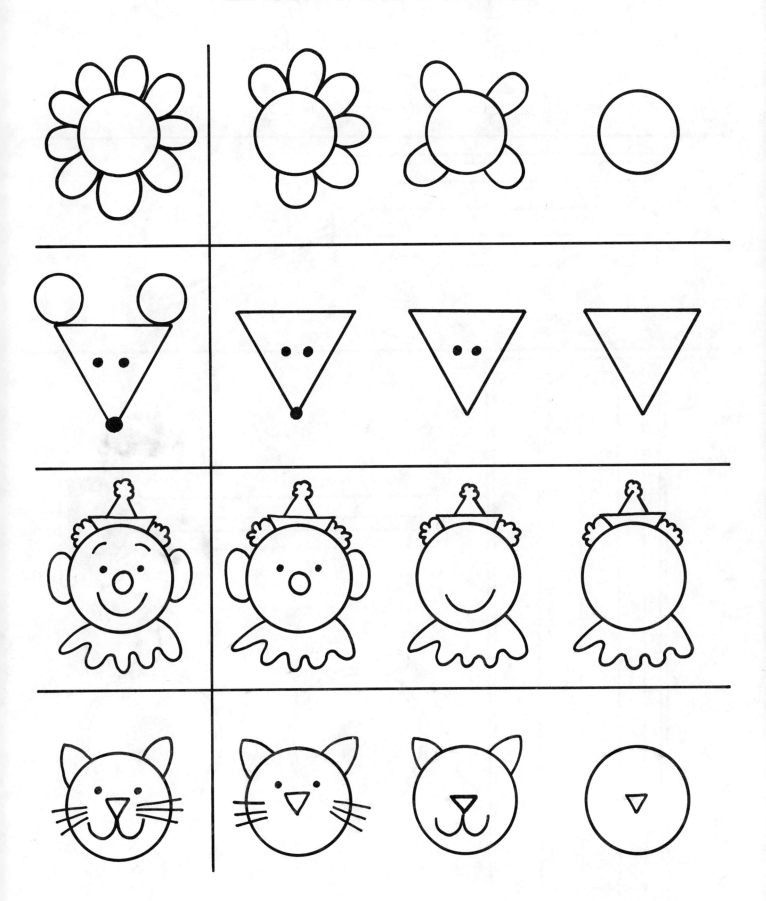

Visual Perception Skills

Make A Wagon

color   Cut   Paste

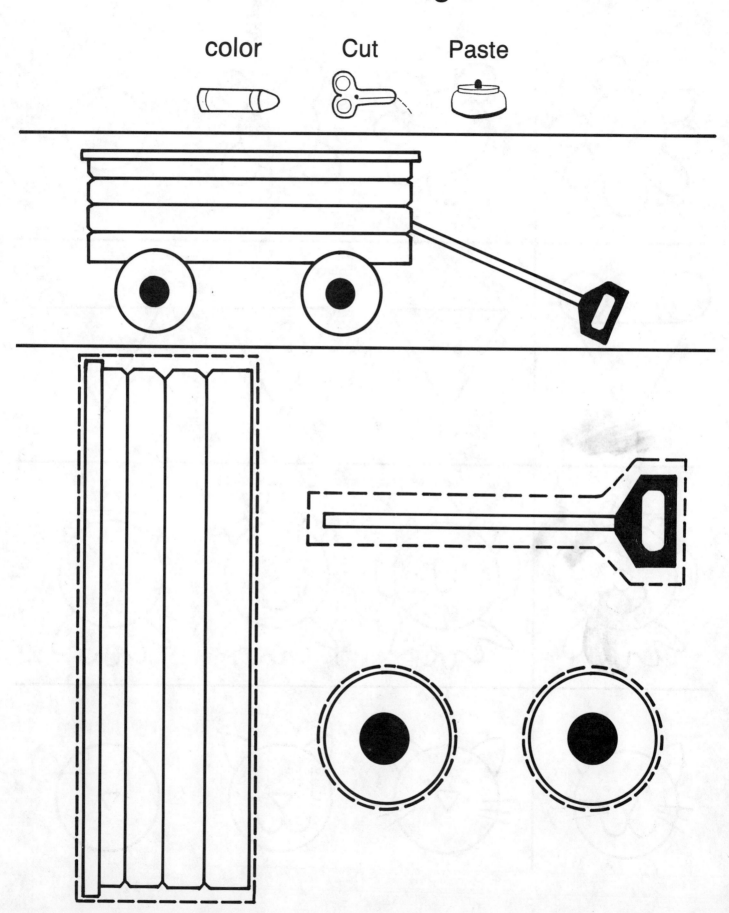

     20   Visual Perception Skills

Make a Squirrel

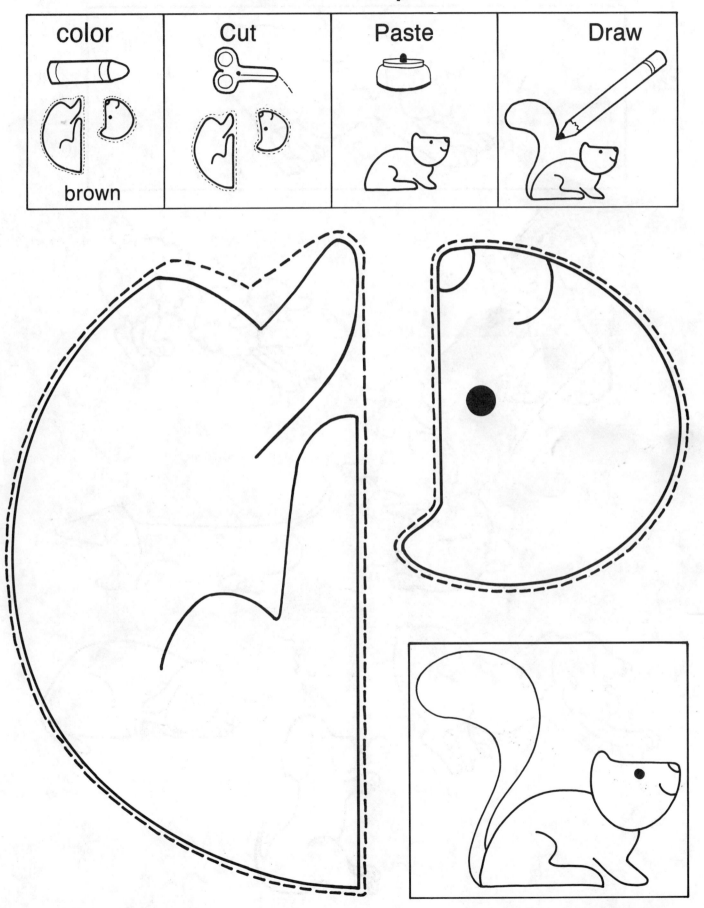

color	Cut	Paste	Draw

brown

Dogs

Copy the Pattern

ABB

ABC

ABCD

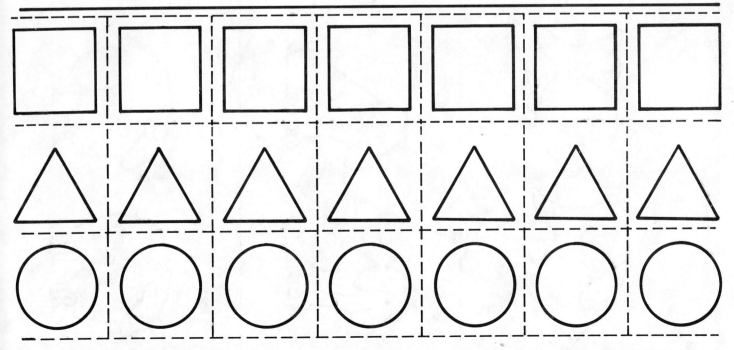

Visual Perception Skills

Copy the Pattern

Teacher: Show an animal pattern card. Children copy the pattern by coloring the animals on their page. This page can be done again by using other pattern cards.

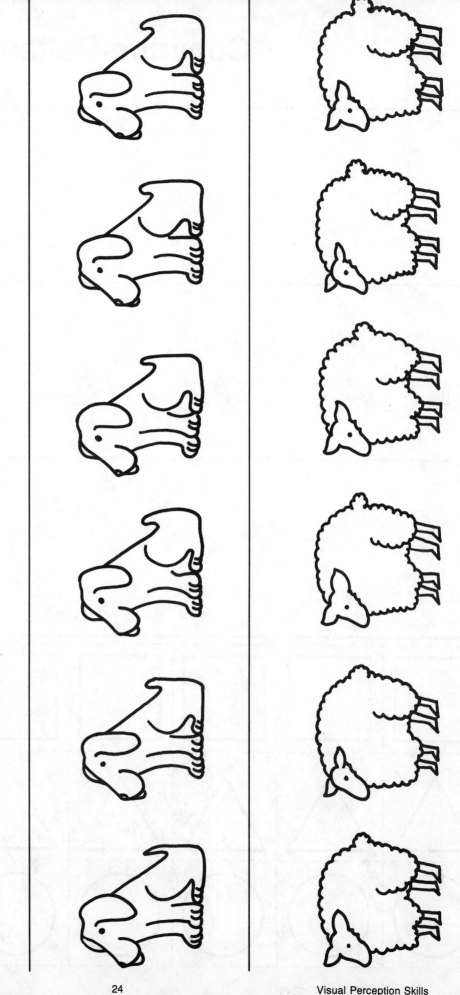

Visual Perception Skills